# HOW TO SLAY
# THE Buffy WAY

# HOW TO SLAY THE Buffy WAY

## Badass Buffy Attitude and Killer Advice

EBURY
PRESS

**Every girl who could have the power, will have the power.**

**Can stand up, will stand up.**

**Slayers every one of us.**

**Make your choice.**

**Are you ready to be strong?**

BUFFY

EPISODE 22, SEASON 7

# Being Brave and Badass

For as long as there
have been vampires,
there has been the Slayer.
One girl in all the world,
a Chosen One ...

— GILES

He loves doing this part.

— BUFFY

**Episode 2, Season 1**

# I'm the thing that monsters have nightmares about.

BUFFY

Episode 11, Season 7

Thank god we're hot chicks with superpowers.

FAITH

Episode 21, Season 7

# SO ARE YOU GOING TO KILL ME, OR ARE WE JUST MAKING SMALL  TALK?

BUFFY

**Episode 1, Season 2**

No weapons, no friends,
no hope. Take all that
away and what's left?

———

ANGELUS

Me. ✝

———

BUFFY

**Episode 21, Season 2**

# I laugh in the face of danger. Then I hide until it goes away.

XANDER

Episode 3, Season 1

# Power.
## I have it.
## They don't.
## This bothers them.

**BUFFY**

*EPISODE 12, SEASON 5*

# MAYBE IF I COULD LEARN TO CONTROL THIS THING I COULD BE STRONGER, I COULD BE BETTER. BUT I'M SCARED.

**BUFFY**

EPISODE 1, SEASON 5

**Maybe it's because of all the horrific things we've seen, but hippos wearing tutus just don't unnerve me the way they used to.**

OZ

Episode 4, Season 4

# You're scared? That's smart.

# You got questions? You should.

XANDER

**Episode 18, Season 7**

YOU HAVE TO DAWN, THE THING IN WORLD IS TO BE BRAVE.

Episode 22, Season 5

# BE STRONG.

# HARDEST

# THIS

# LIVE IN IT.

# LIVE.

BUFFY

**And what are we if not women up to a challenge?**

BUFFY

**Exactly. I mean, did we not put the 'GRR' in 'GIRL'?**

WILLOW

EPISODE 2, SEASON 4

# You wanna surprise the enemy?

## Surprise yourselves.

## Force yourself to do what can't be done.

---

BUFFY

# Mist.
# Cemetery.
# Halloween.

# Should end well.

**GILES**

*EPISODE 6, SEASON 6*

# Saving

# the

# World

I SUDDENLY FIND MYSELF NEEDING TO KNOW THE PLURAL OF 'APOCALYPSE'.

---

RILEY

**Episode 12, Season 4**

I'm not exactly quaking in my stylish-yet-affordable boots but there's definitely something unnatural going on here, and that doesn't normally lead to hugs and puppies.

BUFFY

**Episode 7, Season 6**

I would love to be
upstairs, watching
TV or gossiping about
boys or even studying!

But I have to save the world.

Again.

Episode 21, Season 2

**If you save the world I'll come back, we'll have drinks.**

**When! When, I mean.**

CLEM

But the world continues to turn.

---
GILES

No one will ever know how close it came to stopping. Never know what we did.

---
WILLOW

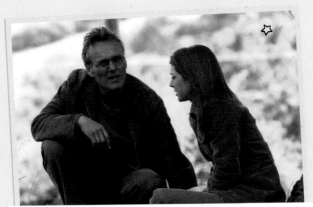

**Episode 13, Season 3**

# 'Destroyer of the universe'. Guess cutting school doesn't seem so bad now, huh?

*DAWN*

**Episode 20, Season 5**

# IF
# APOCA
# COMES,

Episode 5, Season 1

**THE**

**LYPSE**

**BEEP ME.**

BUFFY

**THEY THINK WE'RE GONNA WAIT FOR  THE END TO COME, LIKE WE ALWAYS DO.**

**I'M DONE WAITING.**

**THEY WANT AN ✝ APOCALYPSE?**

**WELL, WE'LL GIVE 'EM ONE.**

**BUFFY**

*EPISODE 10, SEASON 7*

# We saved the world.

# I say we party.

**BUFFY**

EPISODE 12, SEASON 1

# Surviving
# School

EPISODE 22, SEASON 2

# CONGRATULATIONS TO THE 🏆 CLASS OF 1999. YOU ALL PROVED MORE OR LESS ADEQUATE. THIS IS A TIME OF CELEBRATION. SO SIT STILL AND BE QUIET.

**PRINCIPAL SNYDER**

# The dead rose! We should at least have an assembly!

XANDER

**Episode 2, Season 1**

I know. If you don't go
out it'll be the end of
the world. Everything is
life or death when you're
a 16-year-old girl.

_____

JOYCE

**Episode 2, Season 1**

**Groping in a broom closet isn't dating. You don't call it a date until the guy spends money.**

CORDELIA

We're proud to say the class of '99 has the lowest mortality rate of any graduating class in Sunnydale's history.

JONATHAN

**Prom speech, Episode 20, Season 3**

# How was school today?

BUFFY

**The usual: big square building filled with boredom and despair.**

DAWN

EPISODE 13, SEASON 5

# Giles lived for school. He's actually still bitter that there are only twelve grades.

## XANDER

**Episode 8, Season 2**

Sweetie, you
wouldn't blow off
a class if your
head was on fire.

_____

TARA

**Episode 19, Series 5**

# You're really campaigning for bitch 👄 of the year, aren't you?

CORDELIA

# As defending champion, you nervous?

BUFFY

I have witnessed a
millennium of treachery
and oppression from 〰
the males of the species
and I have nothing but
contempt for the whole
libidinous lot of them.

_____

ANYA

So why are you
talking to me?

---

XANDER

I don't have a
date for prom.

---

ANYA

**Episode 20, Season 3**

**Guys. Take a moment to deal with all this. We survived.**

OZ

# It was a hell of a battle.

BUFFY

# Not the battle. High school.

OZ

EPISODE 22, SEASON 3

# Falling in love

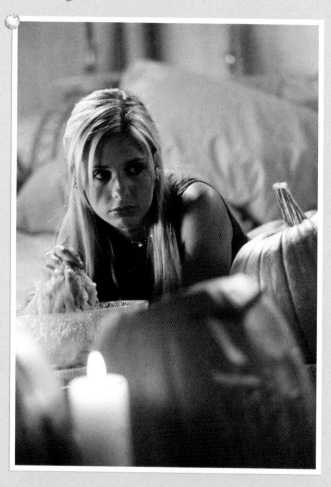

**Episode 6, Season 2**

Dates are things normal
girls have, who have
 time to think about
nail polish and facials.
You know what I think about?

✧   Ambush tactics.
✧ ✧ ✧   ✧   Beheading.

BUFFY

# So you're feeling better about Angel?

WILLOW

Well, we talked. And then he ripped the heart out of a demon and fed it to me. And then we talked some more.

BUFFY

EPISODE 18, SEASON 3

It used to be simple.

A hundred years,
just hanging out,
feeling guilty;
it really honed
my brooding
skills.

Then she comes along.

ANGEL

EPISODE 7, SEASON 2

If you don't wanna fight, you don't fight. You don't use magic to make the fight go away.

TARA

**Episode 8, Season 6**

Anya, this is crazy.
We had a little fight.
That just means that
we have to work our way
through some stuff.
It doesn't mean we rebound
with the undead!

---

XANDER

**Episode 7, Season 6**

# The day you suss out what you do want, there'll probably be a parade.

## SPIKE

**Episode 18, Season 4**

# YOU THINK HE'S TOO OLD BECAUSE HE'S A SENIOR? PLEASE!  MY BOYFRIEND HAD A BICENTENNIAL.

**BUFFY**

*EPISODE 13, SEASON 2*

# A vampire in love with a slayer.

# It's rather poetic.

# In a maudlin sort of way.

GILES

**Episode 11, Season 1**

**Are you mad at me for being around too much, or for not being around enough?**

ANGEL

**Duh, yes!**

BUFFY

EPISODE 21, SEASON 3

Why waste time being all shy and worried about some guy and if he's going to laugh at you? Seize the moment.

Because tomorrow you might be dead.

———

BUFFY

**Episode 1, Season 1**

She wouldn't even kill me.
She just left.
She didn't even care enough
to cut off my head or
set me on fire.

Is that too much to ask?
You know, a little sign that
she cares?

_____

*SPIKE*

**Episode 8, Season 3**

# Men can be such jerks sometimes.

# Dead or alive.

**WILLOW**

EPISODE 17, SEASON 2

# Without passion we'd be 🕊 truly dead.

ANGEL

Episode 17, Season 2

Do you know what the saddest thing in the world is?

_____

DARLA

Bad hair on top of that outfit?

_____

BUFFY

To love someone who used to love you.

_____

DARLA

**Episode 7, Season 1**

I've seen your
kindness, and your
strength, I've seen
the best and the
worst of you and
I understand with
perfect clarity
exactly what
you are.

You're a hell
of a woman.
You're the
one, Buffy.

———

SPIKE

**Episode 20, Season 7**

# I LOVE YOU. NOTHING CAN CHANGE THAT, NOT EVEN DEATH.

**ANGEL**

*EPISODE 13, SEASON 3*

# I know you'll never love me.
# I'm a monster.
# But you treat me like a man.

˯˅˯˅˅˅˅˅˅ SPIKE ˅˅˯˅˅˅˅˯˅˅

**Episode 22, Season 5**

# Fighting Your Demons

Death is on your heels baby and sooner or later it's going to catch you.

# To kill without remorse is to feel like a god.

◈ ANGEL ◎

**Episode 15, Season 3**

Look, we don't want trouble, you don't want trouble.

_____
WILLOW

Actually we do want trouble. We're demons. We're pretty much all about trouble.

_____
DEMON

**Episode 2, Season 6**

# You have a plan?

GILES

# I am the plan.

BUFFY

Episode 7, Season 4

# People ... They're not even animals, they're just meatbag slaves to hormones, pheromones and their feelings.

GLORY

EPISODE 21, SEASON 5

**Vampires
are
creeps.**

BUFFY

**Yes, that's why one slays them.**

GILES

EPISODE 11, SEASON 2

I've sworn to protect this scary world, and sometimes that means saying and doing what other people can't.

They shouldn't have to.

———

GILES

**Episode 22, Season 5**

# This is my lucky stake.

# I have killed many vampires with it.

# I call it 'Mr Pointy'.

KENDRA

I FEEL LIKE
STAYING IN.
AND DOING MY
HOMEWORK.
AND FLOSSING.
AND DYING
A VIRGIN.

WILLOW

**Episode 16, Season 3**

**Oh poor Watcher. Did your life pass before your eyes?**

**Cup of tea, cup of tea, almost got shagged, cup of tea ...**

SPIKE

EPISODE 1, SEASON 6

# Looking Out for Your Friends

I know you're about to do something apocalyptically evil and stupid, but hey, I still want to hang.

XANDER

EPISODE 22, SEASON 6

If it's guilt you're looking
for Buffy, I'm not your man.
All you will get from
me is my support.

And my respect.

_____ &d

GILES

**Episode 14, Season 2**

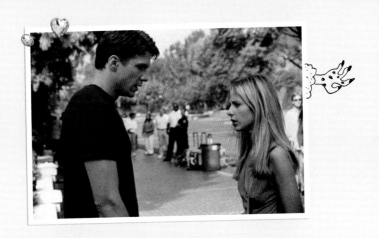

Things fall apart, Buffy.
And evil – it comes and goes.

But the way people manage is
that they don't do it alone.

They pull each other through.

**Episode 11, Season 4**

**Whatever you choose, you've got my support. Just think of me as ... as your ... You know,** 🩲 **I'm searching for supportive things and I'm coming up all bras.**

XANDER

EPISODE 19, SEASON 5

To forgive is an act
of compassion, Buffy.
It's not done because
people deserve it.

———

GILES

**Episode 19, Season 2**

You're not friends,
you'll never be friends.

You'll be in love till
it kills you both.

You'll fight and you'll shag
and you'll hate each other
until it makes you quiver.

But you'll never be friends.

SPIKE

**Episode 8, Season 3**

I just didn't
want to
put you in
that kind
of danger.

BUFFY

**As opposed to the other kind we're always in?**

XANDER

EPISODE 13, SEASON 5

# Finding
# Your
# Way

# STRONG IS

# IT'S HARD

# PAINFUL

# EVERY DAY

# WE HAVE

Episode 10, Season 3

# FIGHTING. AND IT'S AND IT'S IT'S WHAT TO DO.

BUFFY

# It's because you don't have a strong father figure, isn't it?

JOYCE

# It's just fate, Mom. I am the Slayer. Accept it.

BUFFY

Episode 21, Season 2

It's terribly simple. The good guys are always stalwart and true. The bad guys are easily distinguished by their pointy horns or black hats. We always defeat them and save the day.

GILES

Liar.

BUFFY

**Episode 7, Season 2**

# You're not special, you're extraordinary.

---

## XANDER

**Episode 12, Season 7**

Something made us different.
We're warriors, we're built to kill.

FAITH

Kill demons! But it doesn't mean
we get to pass judgement, like
we're better than everyone else.

BUFFY

**Episode 15, Season 3**

# In the end, we all are who we are, no matter how much we may appear to have changed.

GILES

**Episode 1, Season 7**

I GOT IT SO WRONG.
I DON'T WANNA
PROTECT YOU FROM
THE WORLD.

I WANNA SHOW
IT TO YOU.

BUFFY

**Episode 22, Season 6**

**The big moments are gonna come. You can't help that. It's what you do afterwards that counts.**

**That's when you find out who you are.**

WHISTLER

EPISODE 21, SEASON 2

# I don't know how to live in this world if these are the choices.

BUFFY

**Episode 22, Season 5**

# FUNNY HOW THE EARTH NEVER OPENS UP AND SWALLOWS YOU WHEN YOU WANT IT TO.

**XANDER**

EPISODE 4, SEASON 1

Sometimes the most adult thing you can do is ask for help when you need it.

∿∿∿∿∿∿

GILES

**Episode 22, Season 6**

Time was, I thought humans existed just to hurt each other. Then I came here and found out that there are other types of people. People who genuinely want to do right. Then they make mistakes, they fall down, but they keep trying.

ANGEL

Nothing's ever simple any more. I'm constantly trying to work it out – who to love or hate, who to trust. It's just like, the more I know the more confused I get.

BUFFY

**I believe that's called growing up.**

GILES

Episode 7, Season 2

# I MAKE IT THROUGH THIS AND THE NEXT THING AND THE NEXT THING, AND MAYBE ONE DAY I TURN AROUND AND REALISE I'M READY.

**BUFFY**

EPISODE 22, SEASON 7

1 3 5 7 9 10 8 6 4 2

Ebury Press, an imprint of Ebury Publishing,
20 Vauxhall Bridge Road,
London SW1V 2SA

Ebury Press is part of the Penguin Random House group of companies
whose addresses can be found at global.penguinrandomhouse.com

Compiled by Liz Marvin
Design by Emily Voller

First published by Ebury Press in 2018

www.penguin.co.uk

A CIP catalogue record for this book is available
from the British Library

ISBN 9781785038761

Colour origination by RHAPSODY
Printed and bound in China by Toppan Leefung

Penguin Random House is committed to a sustainable future
for our business, our readers and our planet. This book is made
from Forest Stewardship Council® certified paper.

MIX
Paper from
responsible sources
FSC® C018179